Latresha, Continue leading in HEARTwork!
Dr. B

KNOW YOUR PLACE RUN YOUR RACE

Meaningful Nuggets for Educators
Who Are Willing to Be Resilient Leaders

KNOW YOUR PLACE RUN YOUR RACE

**Meaningful Nuggets for Educators
Who Are Willing to Be Resilient Leaders**

DR. KACY SHAHID

MISSION
POSSIBLE
PRESS

Mission Possible Press
Creating Legacies through Absolute Good Works

The Mission is Possible.

Sharing love and wisdom for the young and "the young at heart,"
expanding minds, restoring kindness through good thoughts,
feelings, and attitudes is our intent. May you thrive and be good
in all you are and all you do...
Be Cause U.R. Absolute Good!

Know Your Place Run Your Race, *Meaningful Nuggets for Educators
Who Are Willing to Be Resilient Leaders*

© 2021 Dr. Kacy Shahid   DrKacyShahid.com

Books may be purchased in quantity by contacting the publisher directly:
Mission Possible Press, A division of Absolute Good
PO Box 8039 St. Louis, MO 63156
or by calling 240.644.2500
MissionPossiblePress.com

ISBN: 978-1-7352454-0-9
First Edition Printed in the United States

Hope you ignite n path - of self discovery 🙏 Dr Kay Shahid

Dedication

To every person that has voluntarily or involuntarily worn the mask of insecurity and self-doubt, I hope this book offers you the courage to be vulnerable and stand in your TRUTH.

*Be courageous and fearless, or in other words, **Intrepid**.*

Acknowledgements

I want to thank my husband Mellve Shahid, Jr., for believing in me, and for supporting and encouraging me to get out of my own way and write this book! To Kennedy, Kori, Kyndal and Mellve III, thank you for your unwavering love, support and encouragement to unwind, have fun and enjoy our home together.

Thanks to my mother, Linda, for establishing a love for learning early in my life; you taught me strength, courage and determination. Thanks to my late father LeRoy for lessons in candor, military prowess and boldness.

To my Central Visual and Performing Arts family -- staff, students, parents and fellow alumni, thank you for shaping me, encouraging my creativity as a student, and for continuing to be foundational to my growth and development as a school leader.

There have been many people of influence throughout my career to whom I am very grateful. To the District Leaders of St. Louis Public Schools, including Sheila Smith-Anderson, Dr. Paula Knight, and Dr. Kelvin Adams, thank you for giving me an opportunity to be an innovative disruptor for my students and staff.

The wisdom, experiences and advice that I have been given is invaluable. Since it would be impossible to name everyone, please accept my sincere gratitude to each person who has taught me through the ups and downs of being new to education and to leadership. Shaire Duncan, thank you for being such a supportive encourager, no matter what; I am proud of your journey and what is to come for your future. Maxine Clark, Dr. Tom Hoerr, Dr. Terry Harris, Dr. Katrice Noble, Dr. Sharonica Hardin-Bartley, and Dr. Ian Buchanan, thank you for modeling servant leadership.

Thank you Ni Rita Bradford for your mentorship, guidance, and example as a lifelong educator and student advocate. Words cannot express how much your presence has changed my perspective and life.

Not only did you encourage me to join our illustrious sisterhood, Delta Sigma Theta Sorority, Incorporated, you also introduced me to your former student who helped me complete this book.

Thank you to Jo Lena Johnson, who sat with me for countless hours asking me questions and listening to me as I struggled to recount the memories of my life. You have helped with the structure and polished this manuscript into a quality book of which I am most proud. You have been more than my writing coach, you have become my friend.

Contents

"Success is to be measured not so much by the position that one has reached in life, as by the obstacles which he has overcome."

~ Booker T. Washington

This quote makes me remember what I went through in my past, those life experiences that have shaped me. Thinking deeply about education and the work we do – we work with lives, it's critical no matter what position we're in that we realize that, so that we are prepared and fortified for *heart* work, not hard work.

AWARENESS

Knowledge or perception of a situation or fact.

Transparency and Cultural Humility

When struggling to do something important,
it's natural to try and fake it, avoid or
go it alone. Yet the sign of a mature and
responsible person is to do what we can, and
get support where we need it.

It has taken 20 years to share my most vulnerable moments. This experience, writing this little book, has forced me to "see me" - with all of my flaws and imperfections that I had creatively camouflaged.

I have a doctorate degree. I am an educator. It should have been easy to whip something up and not feel exposed or emotional, especially since it's a book for my fellow educators, right??? It was not. It's easy to give advice, much more difficult to admit to mistakes, missteps and internal motivations. And, quite transparently, finding the time to actually sit down and write a whole book by myself. Once I admitted I would be retired before that happened, I finally decided I would *ask for help* - something that is not necessarily natural to me. I got creative and hired a writing coach.

Why would I need a writing coach? I'm glad you asked.

It is very challenging sharing intimate parts of yourself with the world. I have learned the importance of transparency. My writing coach pushed me to write from an authentic and genuine place. I made several attempts to derail the process by suggesting certain portions of my life were irrelevant or insignificant. I would worry about what others would say or think, so I didn't want to share them.

Today, I now know that every experience and situation I encountered has helped to shape and mold me into the woman, mother, sister, school leader, and wife I am today. Many students I serve have been exposed to traumatic situations and are looking to me and others for help. *Your students look to you.*

We must learn to share and work together, in order to fulfill our responsibilities.

It is our responsibility to inform, teach, and inspire our future generations and to model what is possible. If I am to continue leading my school, prioritizing this notion of being trauma informed, then I must too model *cultural humility*, and so must we all, in our unique and individual ways.

Cultural Humility is a humble and respectful attitude toward individuals of other cultures that pushes many to challenge their own cultural biases, realize they cannot possibly know everything about other cultures, and approach learning about other cultures as a lifelong goal and process.

My hope in sharing *Know Your Place Run Your Race, Meaningful Nuggets for Educators Who Are Willing to Be Resilient Leaders*, is to offer the novice school leader, millennial educator and enthusiastic teacher, practical nuggets and strategies that have been helpful to me over my professional and personal career.

In these years of failures and success, I have found the courage to share my story. Please use what you glean here to fortify you in your own professional and personal endeavors - for the students, and for you!

Thank you!

Dr. Kacy

Heart Work

If educators desire longevity in the field, it requires "Heart work."

Heart work is the part of us beyond our human selves – it's the inner knowing, strength and connection that draws us to the work in the first place, and it's the work that keeps us here when we feel overwhelmed, helpless, angry or worn out. I have *surrendered to vulnerability*, chosen to live in *transparency, learned to confront fear, and continue to overcome judgment – it's taken me over 20 years to get to this point. And now it's time to provide you and others encouragement by offering hope, rationale and strategies to fortify you, the leader, the educator and the PERSON.*

Personally, I believe I have a mission and calling for Heart work. However, some may not be called, but they have accepted the mission. The work of educating young people requires patience, optimism and a relentless focus to impart knowledge, evoke change, serve, inspire, motivate and to stay engaged in the mission. This mission is not for the weak or faint. But it is for those who truly believe all children can learn. (Even on those days we want to give up).

There is a community of us, with shared experiences, that often go unaddressed because we only share portions of who we are. We don't present ourselves as human beings – we share the parts that make us look good. We share our great lives and wonderful pets more than sharing stories of our own families and children. And I get it; it's dangerous sharing too much, but if we never share about our own experiences, then we're unable to support our colleagues. We'll find ourselves standing in a place of judgment versus a space of service.

As educators, it's embarrassing and taboo to admit that our own families have issues. Our own children may be failing in school, suffering with illnesses or struggling with substance abuse. We may wear the diamond rings, but suffer in silence as our marriages or relationships exhaust, strain or deplete us. We often ignore our mental and physical health. We put on the mask, and confide in no one, and we continue to exist, without a plan of action for our own stuff.

Why does this happen? Because we are teachers/educators, we have this all-knowing mentality, so we never want to share our failures – we want to start at the good part. We end up lacking empathy and compassion for our students, parents and fellow teachers because we wear the mask. We would rather pretend our lives are perfect. When we do this we aren't being honest, reflective or transparent. Therefore, we stunt our growth.

My hope is that the strategies and nuggets found in this book are resources you can put in your toolbox and use. They probably won't be new things that you haven't heard; (we know physical exercise is important) however, when was the last time a teacher was told to go get some therapy? You may need it! (Like yesterday!) It's time to take off the capes and masks, just like I'm doing now... and get whatever help we need, so we can stay in this profession. The future depends on us.

I want to share my experiences – the good and bad- and hope you will avoid some of the pitfalls I've experienced; hopefully you can learn from some of the successes. It took me a while to learn certain things. If I could go back twenty years ago with some of these lessons, I'm confident that life would have been much easier.

Especially in education, it's easy to work in isolation and to forget what it was like to be a beginning teacher, or a novice school leader... This work requires a support system and plan.

There's somebody somewhere ready to give up and we cannot give up – we have a whole generation looking up to us and it's our duty to remain steadfast.

We are nation builders. The future depends on us. Being dependable means being healthy in every aspect of life, including physically, mentally, and emotionally.

TRAUMATIC CHILDHOOD EXPERIENCES

Student suicide rates are at an all-time high in this fragile time in America.

We, as educators, now know that many students experience trauma. What are we going to do about it?

Instability Creates Devastation

*Students are often at-risk in the midst of
the family's overall struggle/dynamics.
Rich or poor, habits and deficiencies of
parents, and the lack of structure can
be equally harmful.*

During the writing of this book, I read the story of teen football star Bryce Gowdy, who faced struggles before his suicide during the 2019 Christmas break, days before he was to begin his full-ride scholarship to Georgia Tech. In the days leading up to him standing in front of a moving train, he was displaying all sorts of red-flag behavior. Yet, his family was homeless, and he was anxious about leaving his mother and two younger brothers behind. The article said that an average of two teens a week commit suicide in Florida. Reading the story filled me with tears, grief and flashbacks.

Suicidal thoughts and depression often have many causes. Social difficulties, stress, academic pressures, and other concerns facing teens may contribute to suicidal ideation. (Verywellmind.com)

Other risk factors include:

- Poor social relationships

- Lack of family support

- Physical or sexual abuse

- Substance and alcohol misuse

- Health issues

- Bullying

How many more kids must die at the hands of suicide and violence before we're proactive and intentional about creating plans of action to address this epidemic?

Parents incarcerated, no homes or beds to sleep in, compromised because of hunger and poverty, in danger of physical and emotional abuse, and we expect kids to come to school, be normal and focus on taking tests.

If we don't address this need for mental health awareness, we will continue to perpetuate the societal ills. We must look deeper and address what kids are exposed to. Times have changed and kids are heavily influenced by social media. We must teach them how to cope.

What could it look like? Sessions dedicated to teaching life and coping skills, healing circles and openly talk about stress and what they are going through. Kids should be free to tap into their emotional needs. There is a need, we don't have all of the answers, and it's not just with students, it's with staff as well. It's important to establish processes and procedures to bring people and resources together, along with community partners to provide social and emotional wrap around services.

My Personal Story

Though my past doesn't define me, I can now admit that it shaped me.

According to the noted American Psychologist Abraham H. Maslow, the most essential of our needs is physiological. He stressed the importance of focusing on the positive qualities in people, as opposed to treating them "as a bag of symptoms."

If we are then to follow "Maslow's Hierarchy of Needs," it is critical for kids to have their basic needs met such as food, water and shelter. When those things are missing, it's nearly impossible to make progress in other areas. As educators and people in general, it's difficult to relate to this because the majority of America's population have not suffered from homelessness or food insecurity. However, many have, including me.

My motivation for discussing this is that unless we are aware that trauma has shaped the lives of some of our students, we can miss the red flags that should be alerting us to the needs and the challenges. And while we can't, alone, fix all of the problems associated with poverty, abuse or neglect that some kids experience, having a greater understanding is an initial step to empathy, compassion, and being able to direct resources in tangible and necessary ways.

The Foundation of My Early Childhood was not "Protective"

My history between birth and graduating high school is a bit difficult to share, not just emotionally, but also because of the events, the circumstances surrounding those events, and also the people in my family, who those events affected.

My goal here is to give you an overall picture of my upbringing in hopes that it gives insight as to the unreported trauma that happens with children, and how it can and does affect every area of their lives. When we have a greater understanding, we can choose to have a greater capacity to address issues -- kids have needs, parents have issues and families suffer because of their circumstances - certain things are not self-imposed, but others are - and then children are left to deal with what has or is happening...

My mom and dad were both from Missouri. They spent about a year together and at some point moved to Iowa, where I was born, the youngest of my mother's six children, and the only one of their union. When things were not going well with their relationship, my dad packed up the family and sent them to my mother's mother in Buffalo, New York. Though my mother expected him to join them, he joined the military instead. For the next few years, my mother, with the help of her mom and siblings, did what she could to take care of the four kids who were in her care.

Foster Care

At one point however, my mother lost custody, and my siblings and I ended up in foster care. I was very young, under five years old, and from what I'm told, the white lady who was my foster mother beat me to the point that I had welts covering my arms and legs. My response had been to ball myself up into a protective cocoon-like shell, be silent and do my best to seem invisible.

At some point, when my dad's family found out that I was "in the foster care system," they were able to take me and raise me for a time, back in St. Louis. My mother worked hard to get us back, and I was returned to Buffalo where I lived with my mom and my sister Denise, who is 11 months older than me.

I was Violated as a Young Girl

Early on, a relative began sexually molesting me, between the ages of five and nine. I "told on him" and a family member "beat him up" for what he did. There was a period where he wasn't around, and I was spared contact with him. Later, he would sneak over when Mom was not at home. He did not penetrate me, nor did he commit more serious acts; however, he did touch me inappropriately and I remember three distinct times this happened. The last time he touched me, I was nine years old.

When I think about the molestation, the word 'confusion' comes to mind. In my mind, I believed male relatives were supposed to protect us, especially as little girls. So the fact that he harmed me was confusing. These experiences also made me paranoid when it came to hugging or being close to anyone of the opposite sex - so early on, my sense of trust regarding men was eradicated.

Leaving Buffalo

Mom worked a lot, but she also instilled in us the importance of school work, getting good grades and good study habits. Before leaving Buffalo, Mom ran a tight ship. The routine was that we take off our school clothes, put our on our play clothes, do our school work, eat dinner at a certain time as a family, and never sit in the living room, where the fancy furniture was located. She gave us extra book reports, made sure that we were good readers, and she even won the School Award for Most Involved Parent when I was in 3rd grade.

My mother started dating a man who would visit in the evenings. We began to hear furniture being knocked around, low moans and my mother begging him to stop hitting her. She tried to hide what was happening behind closed doors but it was useless; we knew he was abusing her. After one particular beating, my mother had my sister and I pack our clothes and the three of us boarded a Greyhound Bus in the middle of the night, bound for St. Louis. We took with us what we could carry. We were done with Buffalo.

Finding a Home In St. Louis

When we arrived in St. Louis, we bounced around for a few months, sleeping on the couches of relatives, until my mom could secure a home for us. After living with my aunt for a time, we moved into the fully furnished rental house of a woman my mother knew. When someone attempted to break into the house, Mom was there, by herself. We were all afraid to stay there but had no choice until we landed in a cute little bungalow in the Pagedale area of St. Louis, through the housing authority. We actually used shopping carts to move all of our belongings from that house to our new home. Yes, including a mattress from one of the beds, rolling nearly a mile, to our new place. I didn't know we were poor, and somehow it wasn't odd to me that we had to move that way, since my mother didn't have a car.

Once in our own bungalow, I enjoyed schoolwork again and was starting to feel a little more "safe." During this time, my sister was connected with her dad and his family. She had started spending more time with them, and I could see that she was reaping the benefits of having a father.

I began to long for a relationship with my father. I wanted a man to protect me, to love me, and to take care of me, like my sister had.

To that point my mother had always said, "You ain't got no daddy, I'm your daddy!" For years, she would say that to all of us. I would cry. At this point, my desire to know my father was even stronger.

I don't got no daddy? I don't got no daddy!? How did I get here Momma?!? It just didn't add up!

I had begun to feel like a little kid walking alone in the woods. It was as if I was walking along in the forest feeling abandoned and afraid that a bear or a big cat was going to get me, because no one was there to protect me. Whenever my sister would come back home, and especially after holidays, she would have toys that mom would make her share with me. She didn't like it, they were hers, but mom didn't have enough money to buy me things like that, so, she forced her to share.

Finding Daddy

I was determined to find my daddy. So, I begged my mother to help me. Pretty soon, she took me to my father's sister's house, my aunt Mae. She immediately embraced me, as did his other siblings. It felt good because I looked like them, I could tell that they loved me, and it actually made me feel connected to them when they told stories of me as a baby. Of course, I was too young to remember that short time, but it didn't matter. They loved me and I loved spending time with them.

When my dad's mother died, he flew in from California, by himself, for the funeral. I was 12 years old the first time I saw him. He drove me around town, bought me a bicycle, a coat, and a couple of outfits. I remember being excited, believing that because I had "found" my daddy, that we would have a great relationship going forward. I even asked my daddy if he could help out my mom at Christmas, explaining that it wasn't fair for my sister to share her toys with me. I was hopeful when my dad went back to his California home.

The Fire

On the first day of my sixth grade year, our home caught on fire. All of our belongings in our cute little bungalow were destroyed. We had to go live with family members. It took my mom many years to get back on her feet after that.

My sister moved to her dad's house, where she grew up. That left Mom and I.

We moved from place to place, trying to find some stability. I was enrolled in a Visual and Performing Arts middle school, where I learned to express myself creatively. Through the arts and drama, I was able to 'turn off' the trauma at home when I was performing, and for the first time, in a long time, I felt better about myself. However, at home, we weren't getting stable... mom's life had taken a downward spiral. By the time I got to high school, we had moved 10 times over three years.

My Dad Returned to St. Louis

I was 14 years old when I met my dad for the second time. I was at the end of my eighth grade year, hurt, vulnerable, angry and a much different child than he had left. I remember seeing him, as if for the first time. I thought he was unattractive. I actually told myself, *He's ugly* and then in the very next thought I was, *I look just like him*. The only real difference between us was that I had hair, other than that, it was as though I was looking at my twin.

I was so happy and angry all at the same time. I remember thinking, *Where the hell have you been all this time?* I remember being a frightened kid, always worried that someone was going to hurt or harm me. That some drunk man was going to try to rape me. Someone was going to get into a fight, and I was going to witness them get shot or stabbed to death...

Somehow, I thought that if my father was there I would've been protected so I was pumped. Then I was so angry and mad because I thought that he didn't want me. *Where had he been these years? Why hadn't he sent money? Why hadn't he brought me to live with him?* I looked at him and wanted to hit him and hug him at the same time.

My mother and I were living in a senior citizens efficiency apartment where my mother and I slept together on her grandmother's couch. I don't know how he found us, but he had. Thinking back, I wanted my father to say, "Come on! I'm taking you out of here." But he didn't. He didn't give me any money nor any gifts. To make matters worse, after his visit, my mother complained that he hadn't done anything for me. The situation was too much to deal with. My tough exterior had already formed, and this was just one more blow that I was too numb to feel.

Looking back, I know my mother did the very best that she could to care for her children, being a single mother. But it didn't feel so great when I got to middle school and I realized that I was poor.

My mother's drug abuse was not a surprise or shock to me. In fact, I thought everybody's parent was smoking crack or snorting cocaine. It was all I saw on television at the time. *"Stop the madness!" "War on Drugs!"* When Ronald Reagan was President, as part of his agenda he started the war on drugs in 1982, so it was widely discussed. Because of my life, I knew the war was real, I was living in the midst of it. I thought every parent was a single parent and was on welfare or food stamps. I thought everyone received new clothes at the first of the month and shopped at the Goodwill or thrift stores in between. That was my reality, and I didn't have role models to show me anything different.

When my dad returned to St. Louis, he didn't give me money and he didn't have any to give. He had gotten divorced from his wife and returned with only a few personal belongings, no job and no car. Not only did I think he was ugly, I had no respect for him. As he started getting stable, he met Dee, his soon to be "new" wife. Though he had six kids, of which I was the youngest, she overlooked that. They fell in love, got married, and created a good home together. Since they were together, I started getting to know them both at the same time. However, getting to know Dee was easier because we had a clean slate, since we didn't have history. She was kind, motherly and fair to me; therefore building a relationship with her was pivotal. She created a buffer between my dad and I, which opened the door to an actual 'relationship' between us.

A New Environment

By my junior year in high school, I moved in with Dad and Dee after Mom and I got evicted.

So into my own bedroom, with a waterbed, I went. I had two 'little' siblings and I was now a big sister. I was welcomed with open arms by my family, yet I felt like an outsider. I asked permission before going into the refrigerator or getting seconds; and I kept all of my belongings very close, and easily packable. I had grown accustomed to moving at a moments' notice. I didn't know how else to be. I also played emotional games with my dad, purposely being obstinate and dramatic, calling myself punishing him whenever I could. I hadn't forgiven him for not protecting me.

Dad had really stepped up, and I hadn't considered how much he did, every day, to support me. Our house was in located in St. Peters, Missouri, a two hour commute from my performing arts high school. My father woke up every morning at 4:15 to take me to the commuter bus station. I had found my village and was determined to graduate from my school - though it would have been easier on everyone if I had simply transferred.

One day during my senior year, my dad sat me down and explained why he had been absent. He explained that though he had wanted to be a family, which is why he moved my mom and her children to Iowa, they couldn't get along and he felt hopeless and helpless about what to do. He didn't want to leave her, her kids, or me, his daughter, destitute, and felt that 'sending' us to her mother was the best alternative.

He then joined the military. And eventually got married and started a new family. In the years to follow, he hadn't told his wife that he had a daughter (me). So when he came home for his mother's funeral, and after the money he spent on items for me, she found out... this, along with whatever else they had going on, led to a divorce. Hence him coming back to St. Louis, seeking me out, and trying to father me the best he could.

After this conversation, I understood and began to forgive, and see him in a different way. I began accepting the way 'he looked' and also respecting him because I realized he hadn't 'just' abandoned me. By the time I graduated high school, life at my home, my Dad and Dee's home, was much more comfortable, and I felt pretty good about myself and my life.

At the time, I didn't know the term 'resilient' yet, that is what those formative years, in retrospect, demonstrated.

Trauma

Trauma is a deeply distressing or disturbing experience.

Trauma was a real thing for me although at the time I wasn't able to articulate that.

What was missing?

1. Trust

2. Safety

3. Stability

4. The Basic Necessities - food, shelter and a safe place to sleep.

5. Parents who are stable and engaged - including the ability to shelter, protect, provide and guide.

6. Resources - behavioral, psychological, social and emotional support - counselors, therapists and social workers. The school must take a proactive role in making connections for families.

There are students who have and are living through traumatic situations - though you, as an educated professional, may or may not be able to relate to their experiences. It's okay that you can't relate. However, being empathetic is imperative.

To be well-rounded, empowered and equipped to deal with our students in the way they need us, we must be trauma-informed.

Students Need

1. Structure/Clear Expectations – Kids need to be given parameters and clear instructions; they desire it, too, though they don't often realize it. Kids typically do well when there

are set routines and procedures, including specific times designated for homework and dinner.

2. To be heard – Kids need to feel heard and know that their voice and opinions matter. Student advocacy is one way to encourage student leaders.

3. Being able to express creativity – When a child is young, free play is encouraged but as the child matures to an adolescent, schools and adults tend to discourage playful and fun moments. Schools and families should encourage "fun" activities such as Family Game Nights.

4. Accountability – Behavioral/Academic Plans should be clear, fair and measurable in order for expectations to be met, and there must be reasonable consequences for inappropriate conduct.

5. To Know that Adults Care – Building relation-ships requires effort and modeling respect, kindness, accountability and standards.

6. Freedom to Learn – Everyone makes mistakes and it is imperative that kids know that every mistake is not fatal. Yet, they need to be encouraged to also strive for excellence. Allowing students multiple opportunities to learn from their mistakes (and achievements) builds confidence and trust.

Being Trauma Informed

I can empathize with this story and this young man, Bryce Gowdy, whom I didn't know. When students are compromised physically, socially or emotionally, they are vulnerable.

I could have been Bryce, committing suicide. His story should remind us that students are often compromised during the two-week long Christmas/holiday break, summers and any time certain at-risk factors exist. In my own life, the holidays typically caused anxiety for me. The holidays reminded me that I didn't have the family structure that I desired. *What kept me sane was my school family.*

I saw us evicted, moving place to place, and struggling to pay bills. It was a tough life. I was so afraid of being molested or raped and people talking about my mother. I thought I was crazy because I internalized everything they said about her, and felt it was about me. My mother called me "the captain" as if I was in charge of things - a gatekeeper of sorts - so while I didn't control things, I looked tough and I sounded like all was well. I learned to lie at that age – acting like everything was okay because "you can't tell our business" and that resulted in very little help from the school or any agency.

How could they help if they didn't know about my situation?

It was hard for the school to determine what I was going through because I kept up with the latest trends, so I looked the part of a stable normal student. My hair was done, I wore decent clothes and the house looked like a decent house... from the outside. All you could see was a big house, but we lived in a tiny kitchenette in the attic.

Though I didn't know we were dysfunctional, I was uncomfortable with the living arrangements, and this caused trauma for me... there were women and men in the boarding house, no other children.

I slept on a cot in the kitchenette, Monday through Friday, when Momma was away working. This is why I feared rape. I was alone and vulnerable.

During middle school, I missed 20 days in one quarter. *What was happening?* I was stranded at my aunt's house, after staying weekends. Momma worked as a maid 24 hours a day Monday through Friday for a wealthy family in Ladue and didn't have a car; however, I would tell people she was a private duty nurse. My aunt would pick me up, but she would rely on my mother to organize a ride back home. My aunt didn't really want me to go back into those living conditions, feeling they were unsafe for me. So I missed a lot of school during that period, and none of my teachers questioned why I hadn't been in class!

Mom would give me money every Friday evening after she got paid. I then had to go to school and try to be normal. I had to sign my own permission slips and I made sure I ate at school. Sometimes Carol and Clyde, the couple across the hall, would feed me. But most of the time I chose to eat junk food, enjoying Suzy Qs, Doritos or Snickers. I got smart and started going over my aunt's house, especially over the holidays. That was part of my survival.

Being Creative was Natural, I Learned to Love Performing

Attending performing arts schools provided "informal therapy" which helped me to survive. It was as if I was in another world. I experienced being in show choir, theatre and living by my stage name, "Ebonic Boclaire," who was a star, a celebrity who could sing and dance, who was going to be the next big somebody!

I also found healing in reading the book *Rainbow Jordan* by Alice Childress. It gave me hope. It was about a 14-year-old girl who was going from foster home to foster home who was a courageous Black teenager. She became my hero and I modeled who I believed she was, as if she was my friend, in the flesh. It was the epitome of girl-power! So as crazy as things were – I could be *Ebonic* or *Rainbow* and transfer energies to be who I needed to be.

I talked on the phone a lot – that was also therapy. I would talk to my friend Niecy all day because she had time too. Her grandmother was raising her, as her mother wasn't around. Her life was much more stable because of her grandma but our situations were similar. So we could talk about our feelings without judgment.

I Was Committed to Performing

I created a whole new family/reality for myself. It started off as a joke, when I told somebody that Bobby Brown was my stepbrother. Then people started believing it. I was creating my space in the celebrity world, so I wrote a letter from "Brother Bobby," mailed it to myself, and showed it off. It was all part of my theatrics.

Concocting things to make people laugh, one day I brought a portable nail station to school acting as if I was a nail tech... charging a quarter to paint people's nails. I couldn't even paint but I told them I could, and people believed me.

The concocting was about seeking attention. Momma wasn't there, I only had the phone, and so I was able to do these things to get the attention I needed. These were survival techniques.

My Favorite Math Teacher

My math teacher took interest. Mr. D. was unorthodox, he didn't use text books, taught us college level math in middle school, and challenged us by using the chalkboard to solve the problems. He said, "The first person who solves the problem on the board gets White Castle." I was determined I was going to get the White Castle every time – and I did. Looking back I was driven by hunger, attention and a spirit of competition. I started getting recognized for being smart.

One year the secretary called me into the office and told me she was going to change my class schedule. They put me in higher level classes. My behavior started changing because prior to that, I was talking back, was disrespectful, and intimidated some classmates. I'm not proud of any of this. But this is how I recognize inappropriate behaviors today. When they are showing signs of attention seeking, rude to others, intimating, talking about other folks, those are indicators that something is going on with that particular child. It's a red flag because they are trying to take the attention off of themselves.

Until the school secretary took an interest in me, nobody else had pulled me aside and said, "You're smart, what's going on with you?"

Mr. D showed tough love – and I won the competitions but when I would be out of order, he disciplined. He would say, "You've got five seconds to get out of my room and four of them are already gone, now get out!" That meant I had one second, and I got put out a lot.

Something magical happened when my schedule changed. I wasn't with Niecy, my cutup partner. When I was with the higher-performing kids, I got focused. They weren't goofing off, they weren't laughing with me, and I didn't want to cut up. I began to focus on my academics and became proud of being smart. I began seeing myself as a role model. I was in eighth grade and had "play daughters." I had to be a good momma, a good example. I took that job seriously. It was not a game.

High School

Over that summer, without the structure of school and my friends, I changed. At the beginning of high school, I started reverting a bit, testing boundaries, talking about the "good kids." I came in with that silly middle-school stuff, and one day I decided to "mock a good student" by doing everything she did. The "bad students" in the back knew what I was doing but the girl, Angel, didn't. Every time she raised her hand, I did. Each question she asked, I asked a question. When she wrote, I wrote. Then something remarkable happened in the class.

The teacher said, "Kacy, will you please take this to the office?"

I think it was the attendance sheet. I remember walking down the hall, entrusted with this piece of paper, thinking, *I love this!* At that time, I didn't realize it was positive attention, but that's what it was. I just knew I was never turning back. I wanted to be a good student. Angel and I became inseparable, and I was able to have a close-up look at her life and relationships. Her relationship with her mom was pretty stable compared to my life. The sense of normalcy was going to the dry cleaners together, they had a grocery shopping system – which store to go to get the meat, the vegetables, and the other items; they had a washer and dryer at home, she had a hair-care regimen, a skin care regimen, I just picked up all of those things.

Also, her sister went to Spelman College so that focus on going to college became a priority to me, as Angel spoke of being like her sister. In turn, that exposure gave me focus for my future. No one in my family had gone to college and I had never thought about going.

The TV show, *A Different World* was out then and between Angel, her sister and that show, I now had direction. I wanted to be like her sister and go to Spelman and major in engineering like her sister, I wasn't original!

This critical relationship taught me stability, regimens, routines, personal hygiene tips and the healthy bond between mother and daughter. It was good to see what they had, but it also created bitterness and resentment within me because of the lack of stability between my mother and me. I'm sure my mother felt pressured because I was now comparing, questioning and challenging my mother to get herself together. In all fairness to her, I know now that Momma was sick and because of this, she was without resources and unable to be parent responsibly.

What Mom wasn't able to give to me, she now gives to my children. I'm really proud of my mother's decision to go to rehab... She has been clean and sober for about 14 years. I think the beginning of my true healing was when she made amends with me, one of the twelve steps. It was then I understood that drug addiction was an illness, and not just her wanting to neglect her children. Not only did she improve her relationships with us, she has also formed loving, healthy relationships with her grandchildren, and for that I am grateful.

What About the Schools?

*Adults have a responsibility to care for,
to provide, to protect, to nurture and to
love children.*

Let's face it, on any given day, educating students can be challenging, yet those passionate teachers and other adults who I call, "Merchants of Hope" remain focused, resilient and steadfast, working to help the kids excel. They give me joy to know that there are caring adults who want to pour into young people. That's why I stay in the profession. I love being able to thought-partner with other adults. Although some districts see kids as data points, there are actual kids behind each data point whose stories go untold. And sometimes they fall through the cracks.

The district and the state are focused on data points that are real but don't address what's really/actually happening with some of our young people – in their lives and communities. So, some of the societal ills are homelessness, addictions, molestation or sexual abuse, incarceration, single parent homes, mental health issues and poverty. The list could go on and on, but because these are deeply rooted issues, schools and districts don't necessarily understand how to address them. And candidly, it's not solely the district's job.

However, so many are affected and they need so much. It would be in our best interests to be aware, informed and partner with agencies and organizations who are equipped to provide wrap around services to those students.

Developmental Levels Matter

One of the biggest obstacles families and schools face is the disconnect from what is happening and what needs to happen to support the student. If a child had been homeless, living in a shelter and had not been enrolled in formal education at the ages of 3-5, starting school at six, that child would face emotional, social and academic issues. His/her needs would be different from a child who has been in schools since pre-k or kindergarten. Identifying and recognizing the root of the challenges is the first step to true support. The school should provide support for the family, and what they can't provide, outside agencies could partner and provide services/framework outside of the scope/limitations of the school.

As educators, schools and districts, we must be welcoming to families while recognizing that when needs are beyond our scope, there are agencies who can fill in the gaps.

We Must Pay Attention

As educators, we shouldn't have all of the responsibility, but we should know who's in the student population. Parents have a responsibility, yet when they cannot or do not have the capacity, skills or ability, it's left to the other adults to do what's needed.

We can get mad because parents aren't parenting and meeting our expectations. When we do that, we get stuck – judging what we see based on physical characteristics, mental models or personal bias – but we can't stay there. Yes, there are parents that go off on the teachers, and we make a judgment; or some parents don't show up; even though they "should meet the expectations," we have to get past it and still equip them with the tools to be successful in life, no matter what. We must look at the needs of the students through an equity lens, we will always err in the best interest of the child when we do that. We're not giving everybody the same thing.

Ask, "*What does this child need to be successful?*" And then work (together) to make room for a plan for success.

Situations Are Different, We Must Be Aware of the Signs And Act

In my case, the school didn't know what I was going through because I was camouflaging everything. However, I wish the school would have asked questions. Questioned my attendance, all of the address changes, had a care-team meeting, asked my mother to come in, and offered her resources. Had someone paid attention to the signs, perhaps I could have had therapy – even back then.

I was taught not to tell our business.

What if schools had made it safe enough to share? And what if schools lessened the unnecessary stress brought on with making data points a priority?

I was carrying so much weight. It makes me wonder, *How many young people are carrying the weight of adult life-situations as teens, today?*

The kids in these unstable home situations have a hard time focusing on academics the way we want them to as educators. It's hard to do homework if you don't have a table to sit at, a home to live in or are hungry.

We all have these students – the red flags are present. Attendance, behavior, fluctuating grades happen, but I think we get so caught up in the business of doing school that we miss that these are real lives, real kids.

How Much Would It Cost Us to Look Through the Eyes of a Child?

Schools are for kids. If we look at school through the eyes of a child, is it possible that we might change procedures in our schools? Will it be changing dress codes? Forcing them to skip breakfast if they are late? Having the school open during the holiday break? Could we have used some of our budget to buy a kid a Christmas present or a care package filled with food over the break?

The educational system has fallen short on supporting our precious cargo, the students. In some cases we refuse to hear or see them. It is imperative that we understand that in order to have a successful learning environment, we must be willing to look through the eyes of our young people. We have to be willing to listen and give them the opportunity to give voice to the causes of their disengagement, displays of rage and defiance as well as recognizing and acknowledging their emotional needs.

Pressure at Home

There's a lot going on at home. We often miss things about certain students until they do something out of the norm. We take the strong kids for granted. Sometimes, they have breakdowns. Sometimes red flags aren't so obvious. The Power of Being Seen – every student should feel valued and recognized – seen. And if Johnny has missed three days, you should notice it on the second day. If Susan comes to school irritable one day, and she's never like that, we should recognize it, because it's not her norm. Some students stress when they have to take tests – anxiety can rise expectedly or unexpectedly. We must be proactive. Modifications can support progress. Work needs to be done.

My teachers are really good and will text me if they recognize behavior out of the norm. It can be tough sometimes but I'd rather us be proactive rather than miss something crucial.

It is a major responsibility of us as educators... this is what we signed up for. We are special beings. It's heart work. It's not an easy task. This is what we are here for. Schools can conduct **Culture and Climate Surveys** (I've provided one in this book) – to learn what staff thinks, what students think, what challenges we face and come up with a plan of action to correct the course. Once we heard from them and now we are forced to address their concerns.

1. Push up your sleeves

2. Have conversations

3. Conduct surveys

4. Analyze the results

5. Address the concerns

Addressing What Matters

Parents matter. Culture matters.
Diversity matters. Equity matters. Inclusion
matters.

After watching the video of Bryce Gowdy's mother recap the details of what led to her son's tragic suicide, I had to have an honest moment with myself. I realized that before I could begin to understand the humanity for the mother, I had to understand my own identity and the ways I have been socialized to interact with the world. Having experienced homelessness, financial struggles and emotional stress as a teenager, I quickly realized the pressure and fear I face daily in exposing my traumatic experiences. My role as an educational leader has challenged me to be more objective and emotionally balanced when dealing with families.

We all play a critical part in developing safe spaces that affirm and validate our most marginalized students. Additionally, we must leave judgment and implicit bias at the door, and think about all the ways we can support families like the Gowdys.

As a result of these tragic situations I am left with several questions that resonated with my spirit:

1. How do we get more parents and community partners involved to build relationships that are rooted in trust and respect?

2. How can schools create welcoming environments for families to be able to partner with teachers and staff for better outcomes?

3. How can we provide professional development opportunities that can be used as leverage for school leaders and districts around emotions, health, diversity, equity and inclusion?

4. How can schools and districts create systems of accountability that move the learning from the professional development settings to a more practical hands on approach?

In my opinion, we must create spaces where students "feel" seen, where they are free to be their authentic selves. There is a moral duty for schools and districts to be intentional about creating spaces that foster a sense of belonging for all students. Our schools and districts must put the focus on equity, student voice, emotional health, parental involvement, and also identify "safe" schools that are free of bias, prejudice and stereotypical views. – *This is no small feat, as that calls for educators and staff to be free of bias, prejudice and stereotypical views.* It also requires them to reflect on their habits and practices and be willing to be vulnerable.

While I am aware that it is not the sole responsibility of the school/districts to address every society ill that plagues are communities/schools, it is our moral responsibility to remain informed and open to such emotional triggers.

Being a trauma informed educator, I have learned that students' anxiety typically stems from the lack of identity safe schools. The time is now for schools and districts to create safe spaces for our most marginalized students to be seen and heard.

NUGGETS

Pieces of valuable information.

Know Your Place, Run Your Race

Educators are held accountable to certain measures, factors and criteria – yet, depending on the subject or category, inequities exist.

We are held accountable and expected to achieve measuring points; that's the nature of our work, as educators. It may be tempting to take it on as an individual, believing that the leader needs to do "everything." This results in burnout and inefficiency, not in productivity. It's important that we keep the team in mind, and ensure that we are all doing it together – there is no "I" in team, as we've heard millions of times.

Working Together Is What We Must (Learn to) Do

If you are not considered "administration" you may feel discouraged, undervalued or as if your experience, opinions or input doesn't matter. I understand this, and it sucks. Somehow, we must start to overcome each issue by working together to address problems or concerns.

If you are a leader, don't fail to develop and collaborate with members of your team. Interpersonal communication skills along with proper preparation and delegation of roles and responsibilities leads to empowerment. If each member of the team is treated with respect, equity and feedback is encouraged, not punished, people are more likely to feel valued, connected and vested in the overall success.

Trust and teamwork go hand in hand, and must be earned and reciprocated.

Awareness and Accountability

The state and district are looking at assessment data, attendance and graduation rates as well as other measurable goals. This is not new to anyone in education, but how we choose to respond individually and as a school affects the outcome of those goals.

That being the reality, ensure that school districts and schools have a clear comprehensive plan in place, holding the responsible people accountable. Seek out support from your district and state where it's applicable i.e. curriculum specialists, assessment office, and human resources. Remember, we have been working in isolation and our first thought maybe "It's all on me." Yes, as an individual, you are culpable. However, accountability and achievability is dependent on the entire team. Which is why burnout can't live and breathe in successful, high performing school environments. We have goals to meet and lives to save.

Educating students, engaging the senses, shaping and molding, encouraging learning, monitoring attendance, addressing discipline issues, and part-nering with parents can be accomplished if each person is given specific roles, proper training, and clear expectations along with feedback as they are empowered to oversee certain schoolwide respon-sibilities.

Positioning begins with awareness, and ***Running Your Race*** means each person/team must be conditioned

and positioned by ***Knowing Your Place***. Being accountable and addressing inequities is what we must do.

Accountability Includes Measures, Environmental Factors and Practices

    a) Attendance Goals

    b) Bully Awareness

    c) Vertical Alignment in Elementary Education

    d) Appropriate and Timely Disciplinary Measures

    e) Equitable Funding

    f) Reading on Grade Level

    g) Gifted Education

    h) Trauma Informed Practices

    i) Influence of Technology on Teaching

    j) Virtual and Distant Learning

    k) Life Skills Training to include Social and Emotional Learning

    l) Mobility/Homeless Student Rates

    m) Graduation Rates and College Acceptance

n) State Test Scores

o) Staff Retention

p) Teacher Attendance

q) Parental Involvement and Advocacy

r) Safe and Orderly School Environment

s) Special Education

t) School Board Governance

u) Community Issues/Societal Ills that Affect the School/District

v) Recruitment and Hiring of Teachers of Diverse Backgrounds and Experiences

w) Legislation around LGBTQ rights and concerns – including gender neutral restrooms, discrimination and preferred pronouns will continue to evolve as we progress.

x) Racial Discrimination and Racial Profiling are historical problems that continue to go unaddressed. In recent years incidents have increased and sweeping them under the rug is counterproductive.

y) Restorative Justice Training for all Staff, including Contractors and Non-Certificated Support Staff (Bus Drivers, Cafeteria Workers, Custodians, Secretaries, Substitute Teachers and Resource Officers).

z) Classroom incidents of insubordination, discrimination and even violence against educators is being captured by cell phones and videotaping. Self-control and restraint under normal circumstances can be difficult and technology intensifies the atmosphere. Addressing student and teacher reactions and responses is necessary.

We must be aware of what we're doing and what we must do if we are to fulfill our commitment and duty to ensure equitable outcomes for the students we serve.

Silos in Education

Isolation causes a person to be or remain alone.

Why Are There Silos in Education and What Can be Done About Them?

There is no debate that education is the key to the future. As technological advancement continues to challenge and create opportunities for post millennial thinkers, districts and schools must be aware of the educational shifts. Educational systems must be able to tap into the potential of the students they serve and prepare them for an ever-changing world. For this to happen school staff members must examine their own mental models and implicit bias. If educators do not disrupt the status quo of their own beliefs, they run the risk of preparing students for a world that does not exist.

There are many silos that exist in schools and they are based on people – the way they think, perceive, believe and behave. It's usually based on experience or bias of some kind. When silos exist, that creates isolation. Much of the isolation is based on factors that include gender, racial, socioeconomic, and even curriculum/content bias and perceptions. In other words, every aspect of education or teaching and learning is affected – including what is taught and how it is presented.

Silos in schools have created a delusional effect on our current educational system. Some educators believe in the, "We are great syndrome." Silos isolate people, ideas and create the mirage that everything is going according to the plan and "all is well."

My school district recently conducted school culture and climate surveys. Students were asked specific questions about the school culture and the responses were varied. More than 75% felt safe and supported while 25% felt indifferent. The reality of the survey was shocking but nonetheless real. When schools conduct these types of surveys they tend to shy away from the results, unwilling to change because "everything is great."

It is important for schools and districts to peel back the layers at the surface in an attempt to disrupt our current perspectives. This will create opportunities for innovative change and positively impact the learning environment.

It's necessary to bridge gaps on all levels, which is typically beyond one person or entity's control. However, it's important to eradicate silos between districts and employees, and between silos and perceptions. Doing so creates a healthier learning and working environment for everyone.

LEADERS

A person who has influence is a leader. Each of us, individually and collectively, have influence. We are all leaders.

Discovering Passion

Early in life, I had no desire to become a teacher or school principal, I wanted to be a lawyer. I think education found me. I always wanted to work with young people and even volunteered in my spare time doing just that. I was watching an episode of the "The Oprah Winfrey Show," and it was about working in your passion. After doing a self-inventory I realized that working with young people was what I loved and, therefore what I pursued. I fell in love with helping, serving and supporting young people.

As a teacher leader, I volunteered, asked questions, supported the vision of the school leadership team and six years later became a principal.

Know your why – the thing that keeps you passionate and focused on your work. When your passion meets your purpose, it activates a part of you that goes beyond the norm or expected. As we grow, we sometimes gain or lose our levels of engagement. If you feel a lull, re-activate! If you have yet to come to the intersection, keep running, you will get there. After all, there's a lane just for you!

"Allow your passion to become your purpose and it will one day become your profession."
- Gabrielle Bernstein

Leadership Requires Vulnerability

Being able to say, "I don't know," is key to your growth as a leader.

Too many times people (leaders) think we know everything – and for some odd reason, we buy into it and think we are *supposed* to know everything.

My first year as a principal, I had to be all-knowing, period. I wanted people to believe that. I drank coffee in meetings, stayed at work until 7 p.m. and always said, "I'll follow up with you" ... all elements of acting "as if," which was just **extra!** (When it should have been **E for Exhausted!***)*

The nights when I stayed late, I told myself I would (finally) clean out my email inbox. I never did. I would call myself working on a report, or preparing for the next day. But none of it was productive, I was just wasting time.

The Reality?

I was unraveling quickly. I would then go home and tell my ex-husband, "I'm not going to be making all of these decisions at work AND at home!" My stress level was at 100% unnecessarily, when I could have said, "I need help."

The ramifications of lacking vulnerability created a false sense or perception of power – I was wearing a mask. I was just trying to be great. I was trying to be what I thought a working wife and mother was supposed to be. I didn't actually know I was acting like *Superwoman*!

I was a fraud to myself. I made everyone believe that I knew everything, and that I was good. But I was living a lie. And that led to my stress level continuing to escalate.

Being Self-Unaware put my life off-kilter and out of balance.

Being Vulnerable Means Sharing Responsibility

Today, because I realize the benefits of being vulnerable, I'm aware, more reflective and able to ask for support while being transparent and a more effective leader. I've learned that by sharing responsibilities, I'm no longer a work-grabber, nor am I as exhausted or ineffective.

I admit that I don't have all the answers, and it's really okay. I also say no – I don't overcommit anymore.

By sharing responsibility, I take care of me – eating better, leaving work when the sun is still out and modeling that self-care for my team (and family). Because if I'm not good for me, I can't be good for the team.

Effective Leadership Requires Vulnerability

1. Does anyone challenge you? Is there someone holding you accountable?

2. Are you open to feedback or constructive criticism?

3. What areas of growth could you work to develop in order to be a more effective leader?

4. Are you willing to be honest with yourself about your needs?

5. Do you need support or guidance? Are you willing to ask for it?

Being vulnerable lifts the stress and creates space for new opportunities, authenticity and productivity.

Leadership by Fear Doesn't Work

You can't scare people into being "good" teachers.

I was a principal at an alternative school for chronically disruptive students, but I still considered them scholars and classified them as the talented 10th in my mind and expected the teachers to do the same. Anyone who was not on that page was not a "good" teacher!!! Poor teachers!

That's when I was using my own experience as the mark of success. Because if I did it, surely they could do it too! I promise you, I told the teachers that too.

What is a "good" teacher anyway? What does that even mean?

I used to say, "Give me your worst scenario. Whatever the kid has gone through, they were teachable. We can fix them. They can be reached." That's it.

My mantra was *"Ain't no mountain high enough, ain't no valley low enough, ain't no river wide enough to keep us from reaching these scholars!"*

The teachers complained that the students were disruptive and disrespectful. They wanted students to be suspended for their behavior (But we were an alternative school so that wasn't realistic most of the time).

Teachers had excuses for everything and didn't take responsibility for their roles as classroom managers. They weren't optimistic. They were negative and there were too many classroom management issues, but they didn't recognize that. They weren't being patient when the kids were making mistakes, and complained about kids talking in class. In addition, complained that their reading levels and math scores were low.

As this was my first assignment as head principal, I thought that by giving us all a reading assignment, the teachers would "get it" about the kids and we would all be transformed, because we would all see how important being a "good" teacher was. I didn't survey them, nor did I ask them if they would be willing to read the book.

It didn't go well.

We were talking about the book "Push" by Sapphire and some teachers expressed how they had a difficult time reading the book. Someone said, "In the first chapter, the student is talking in broken language and using profanity, so I stopped reading the book."

Others nodded in agreement.

I was outdone!

I felt like, if you can't read this book, how can you see our students?

Things were not going the way I planned!

I needed to take drastic action!

Kacy Joe Clark!

The chair was on the table. I guess the custodian had left it there. I said, "If you can't read this book, how can you see our students?" and for effect, I added, "Just as sure as this chair is here, our kids are too!" I pushed the chair onto the floor as a demonstration of how we tend to throw kids away.

Well, that scared them alright!!

Nobody expected me to do that. At the time, I thought the drama would wake them up, I thought I was jamming.' I was like, "I got 'em! They are going to see these Black kids today!"

Well, it was an epic fail because I scared them instead of jolting them...

What I realized was that I lacked empathy. Though the teachers did lack cultural responsiveness, it was deeper than just reading a book about a Black girl from the inner city. I really thought that if they read the book, see that kid, and then in turn see the students, they could build these perfect relationships.

It sounds crazy now, but that's what I thought.

So when one of the teachers quit a month later, I was surprised. But looking back on it, I shouldn't have been surprised. I didn't support her in the whole idea of her being a Caucasian woman and the cultural gap that existed. At the time I thought they needed rigorous, engaging instructional strategies. I got mad at her for quitting, then I cried. I was really mad at myself knowing that I hadn't done what I could to support her.

I didn't know how to support her or the other staff – I didn't know how to support any of them in building authentic relationships with kids.

I didn't understand that there were levels to building authentic relationships.

Expecting that it was easy or natural for my teachers wasn't realistic, because those authentic relationships didn't exist between us as educators. We lacked experience and trust – it was going to take time – I can say that now, but had no clue then.

So the same way I wanted teachers to scaffold instruction, I had to help them to scaffold expectations, bridge gaps and create strategies they needed to build relationships with students (and with me!)

It was easy for me to get to know the kids. It should have been easy for them as well, right?

The teachers felt I was too "student centered" and that I wasn't holding the students accountable, so the students "liked me more."

I didn't pay attention to those rumblings at the time. Looking back, I had so much to learn. I needed a foundational relationship with the teachers that didn't exist, not to mention all the other things that didn't go well.

In reflection, I had forgotten what it was like to be a teacher.

I wanted them to get the skills I thought would make them "good" teachers. They needed to build relationships with the kids, and I expected that they could just love the kids and everything would come together.

The pieces I missed were asking:

- What do you need from me?

- How can I support you?

- Validating them when things were going well.

- Listening.

I should have offered:

- Mentors

- Coaching

- A Listening Ear

Principals cannot lead with fear. We must lead with empathy, and that means being willing to admit our own shortcomings. We must be communicative, empathetic and compassionate.

These are not just words - this is absolutely imperative. We must also hold students accountable - so much so that teachers know that "the principal" supports them. Under no circumstances is it okay for the students to "like me" and "disrespect you."

Being just and fair must be across the board - and that leads to equity.

> *Honing the skills to be a fair, equitable and patient school leader who cares for, supports and **teaches** is truly a marathon, not a sprint.*

What Does Effective Leadership Mean?

"Leadership is not about being in charge, leadership is about taking care of those in your charge." ~ Simon Sinek

What if your teachers decided not to come to work for the day? What would you do? Gather all of the students in the gym and then become the teacher for the day, looking real silly? You may laugh or cringe, and then maybe you'll realize how important your staff really are.

We can't do the work by ourselves so we have a team of individuals who can assist us in the heart work of educating and developing young people. Choose your leadership team wisely. Pick people who have a different skillset than you. It's imperative that leaders prioritize recruiting, retaining, supporting, developing and building leadership capacity. Effective leaders must put the team first.

You don't have a choice – you must treat your team with respect and kindness because they are essential and the organization cannot function without them. You need them – always remember that.

- Give credit to your team.

- Celebrate and recognize the team members.

- Talk to the team members who are struggling.

- Express gratitude.

- Take responsibility when things don't go as planned.

Effective Leaders Build Leadership Capacity

I remember starting my career as a building substitute teacher. My principal at that time treated me like I was a certificated teacher and allowed me opportunities to be a leader. I was the Distributing Education Clubs of America (DECA) Coordinator, which is a student marketing club. I was also the professional learning community teacher leader which meant I led weekly meetings with a group of teachers as we discussed topics around student behaviors in the classroom, how to keep kids engaged in lessons, and how to use testing data to drive instruction, for example.

I appreciated being assigned these roles and learned from them. Being the Professional Learning Community leader was a great opportunity because I learned about the challenges that teachers faced. By listening to their concerns, my own perspective broadened, and I know hearing their stories helped me to be more empathetic and become a better listener. Yet being in those positions added more work to my daily responsibilities, and I found myself struggling at times to fit it all in.

My principal trusted me in those positions and by doing so, that built my confidence, helping to shape and prepare me for the work of becoming a school leader.

Effective Leaders Create Opportunities for the Team

- Delegate - Allow staff to share leadership responsibilities - doing so empowers them and builds confidence and capacity.

- Build Team Member Skills – Find professional development or other trainings that build the skills and talent.

- Communicate Successes and Challenges – Be candid and transparent to build trust. It takes being vulnerable. The lack of vulnerability hurts the team.

If we don't know we are struggling, we can't do anything about it. It starts and ends with you.

Stay in Your Lane, Know Your Position

I needed to do something drastic! I wanted to create a new vision for myself, one that others would buy into, so I saw myself with a white dress and halo, and decided that I wanted to be seen as angelic.

Kacy the Angel

Since I wanted people to see me as Dr. Angel, I decided to change my vocabulary. I started calling everyone Sweetie Pie, Pumpkin, Honey Bun, anything I thought was sweet. And I changed the inflection of my voice, thinking that they would see me differently. The kids even started saying, "What's wrong with you?" "Why are you talking like that?" My throat even started hurting, as I tried to make my voice sound lighter and laughed more. I wasn't trying to be condescending. I just thought if they saw me that way then they would think I was nice and do what I asked them to do, whether they were teachers or students.

The adults kind of chuckled, seeing through my short-lived attempt to change the perception of who I was. Yet it was the kids who reminded me that I seemed disingenuous – and more importantly, that they liked me for who I actually was.

This is all part of learning who you are as a leader, and also knowing your position in your organization. Some leaders are very compassionate, some are known to be direct and caring, some are very stern, yet *who you are* shows up in the organization.

No matter your position, or what role you play, everyone is a Leader.

We are all leaders of our lives, though we may or may not have a "leadership" title or salary in an organization. When we see ourselves and others as leaders, it makes it easier to hold ourselves accountable, responsible, and it puts us in the mindset for effective positioning.

Everyone's Position is Critical to Winning the War

Staying in your lane and knowing your position is how armies and teams work together to win battles, and ultimately win wars. Each member of the force is trained for a specific function and possesses certain skillsets. They are then tasked with and expected to hold those positions. When this occurs, victory is more likely to happen because capacity has been built based on trust, confidence, knowledge and shared experience. Similar to armies, schools too should have a clear vision and realize that we are on a mission to educate and prepare students for life, living and success.

When you are aware of your strengths and weaknesses, it's much easier to be effective as a team. Being self-aware allows each member of the team to treat, address, solve a problem, refer or hand off what's appropriate, on a daily basis.

If a student is sent to my office because the teacher is concerned they are suicidal, I don't try and "treat" the student. I call in the social workers because they are the persons to deal with the situation - I become support, but they are the one with the skillset, background and experience to navigate toward helping that student. Oftentimes as educators, we forget that teamwork is what is needed, especially in times of crisis.

Everyone Will Not Like You

Being Dr. Angel did not work for me. It's okay that everyone will not like you. We all have to come to that conclusion because every day you are an educator, you will run into someone who does not like a decision or choice you make.

I had a former assistant principal who sent me a message because he was stressed with people not liking him once he made the transition from being a teacher to an administrator. Recognizing that some of the teachers were not being consistent with the way they were treating students, he decided to create a professional development workshop to help them change their patterns. His efforts were commendable; however, because he was younger than most of the teachers and new to the environment, they turned on him. He sent me this message:

"I still struggle with wanting people to be my friend and I need to get over that. I challenged some teachers about making some decisions with kids in mind. My Principal has backed my decisions but now two of the teachers hate my guts."

He was in a tough spot. Things like this happen quite regularly because of culture and tradition, not to mention silos. I responded by saying:

"You cannot challenge teachers and they still will NOT like you. It comes with the territory. Your allies will be the teachers that were like you! Find the teachers that care about kids...they will shield you from the haters! Good overshadows bad all day!"

He wrote me back, and we continued to touch base for a while until he was comfortable standing up for the students while keeping the teachers accountable. They still don't "like him," however, they are treating the students more equitably. Good for him, and good for any of you who may be able to relate to a situation like this.

Leaders Must be Willing to Develop Our Skill Sets and Evolve

The way to achieve this is to do the work with objective professionals who will speak up, tell the truth and support you in altering or developing ways to be effective. It's important to be proactive, not reactive. As leaders, we must acknowledge that we don't know it all, and that we have to continually improve.

At what point do you need a coach/therapist/ accountability partner? You should not have to wait until something "bad" happens. You need the support of those who have the background and experience to help you throughout the race, not your spouse or significant other. Leaders need to take action in order to be effective.

We don't know it all. Admit where you have short-comings. Ask for what you need. Don't allow fear or something else to stop you from reflecting and taking action. Participate in activities that are self-reflective. Be willing to correct any communication issues, perceived power/ego issues, personality style conflicts or other shortcomings.

*Honing the skills to be a fair, equitable, patient adult who cares for, supports and **leads** is truly a marathon, not a sprint.*

*Knowing your place, means knowing which race you're in... the **hurdles** require different conditioning than the long jump.*

BALANCE

An even distribution of weight enabling someone or something to remain upright and steady.

Unbalanced

Being tightly wound is a common way of being for many educators. It produces unnecessary anxiety that we allow. Stressing for no reason doesn't work. We have to learn to be in the flow and adjust when needed.

Work-life balance does not exist. So if you are searching for it, stop wasting your time and refocus your energy. Learn to be flexible and deal with things as they come. It will help you relieve a certain amount of stress, and find the time to enjoy aspects of your life you may have ignored or that have gotten out of balance.

At School

Small things will happen. There will be times when the copy machine is broken, the bells don't work, the intercom is full of static, lunches are late, the fire drill happens in the middle of a test, the weather prevents recess, the buses are late or the internet is down. I've seen some of my teachers stress because these events interrupted the schedule. All of these unplanned distractions can be frustrating, but they shouldn't prevent you from teaching. It's not the end of the world.

Real traumatic events occur. A student has a seizure in the classroom. Everyone is traumatized. The school gets a bomb threat, that's scary, everyone is unnerved and the entire day is disrupted. The teacher's dog or cat is having surgery and now the teacher misses a couple of days of work. Even when these types of traumatic events come up, we still have to be flexible and cope with the interruption. No matter the severity of the incident, we have to control our emotions and anxiety to the best of our ability, for the students, staff and for ourselves. When we don't, that anxiety and stress we evoked on ourselves, the students will feel it. They breed off our energy. When we are calm and rational, they tend to follow our lead.

Flexibility – the quality of bending easily without breaking.

Every situation that might compromise our scheduled events or activities is not detrimental to our overall ability to be effective.

Being tightly wound and unable to adjust when things happen – that's typically about our emotional responses. Learning to control our emotions is half of the battle.

Think, "*What's the Worst That Can Happen?*" And Plan For That.

When those unexpected events occur, if we are proactive in planning other activities, we can use those as back-ups if we don't have needed materials or copies.

If a student's sibling died three days before, when they show up in your classroom, they are likely emotional. When our students experience traumatic events in their families/communities, it affects everyone. When the child returns to the classroom, other students can become curious and emotional. Discussions naturally start to happen, and the teacher tries to interject. Things can really spin out of control at this point. Teachers should not try and deal with the loss alone. I suggest that we rely on our support staff and care team, referring the situation to trained professionals, the social worker, counselor and/or the school administrator.

After the kids have been engaged, we need to have therapy/counseling as well. Most of the time, we don't think about this, consider it or do it. But we (meaning all adults involved) need support. If you don't know a specific person to speak with, you can contact the employee benefits services department of your organization.

Be Proactive and Accountable

Some issues will be one-off or short term inconveniences. When they happen, just breathe, adjust, address them and fix it. Focusing on what's important is less stressful and more productive.

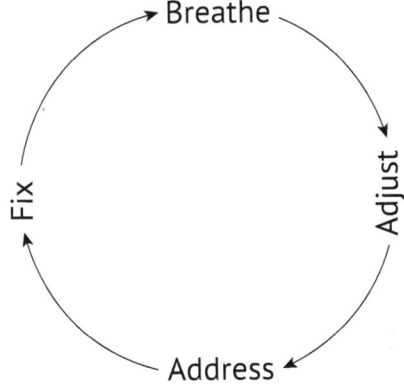

However, when it comes to the systemic issues that challenge your schedules, if they are recurring and problematic, speak up and either offer solutions to the building administrators or the district.

If *you* are the building administrator or the district, address the problem immediately, acknowledge what is being done to address it and solve it. If the matter can't be solved in a timely manner, be willing to explain to the team what is happening. People can adjust better when they are informed.

At Home, Our Personal Lives

As educators, we are who we are. We tend to like routines and schedules. We love our planners and our calendars. And let's face it, some of us are perfectionists. Trying to live a perfect life doesn't exist. If you will wrap your mind around this, it will help you have a better quality of life.

The reality is, perfectionism can be a sign of mental illness. I actually paused when writing this and started to erase it, but no, you need to face it. In education, we live in a "system of perfectionism" that should be challenged, but that we don't have control over. So, I am challenging you to remove that expectation from your home life at least. Being less self-critical and being kind to yourself will release you from the rigidity of perfectionism.

It will be healthier and much more pleasant for you and for those you love.

As educators, we're often so scheduled that we don't have flexibility for ourselves and for our joy. Being tightly wound can cause more stress than finding flexibility, and doing things out of your comfort zone can make all of the difference. Do random things you wouldn't normally do throughout the week.

It is okay if the house is not cleaned every single Saturday. It's okay if you do laundry two days late. It is okay to let your kids eat fast food every once in a while. It is okay if you did not follow the schedule because something enjoyable came up and you decided to attend or participate! Be flexible like a straw; be willing to bend.

Joy is a feeling of great pleasure and happiness.

Joy is a way to experience balance within yourself. Do you know what brings you joy? Do you (still) have hobbies? When was the last time you had a belly-laugh? Do you schedule fun on your calendar?

Change your focus. Focus on the things that find you joy and peace – and participate in them!

So, my advice is the same – be willing to adjust when events occur that don't fit into your schedule. And it's okay to have an adult beverage every now and then – even on a weekday!

Do what increases your confidence, bolsters your esteem, and enjoy your flexibility.

Be in the flow and adjust when needed.

Promoting Self-Efficacy

*If one lacks self-knowledge, they don't often
have the courage to address what's happening
or what's lacking.*

Some people became teachers because they were good students, however, they may lack self-efficacy, which affects communication, the ability to teach, their ability to accomplish goals and perform certain tasks.

Some people lack experience, or are simply introverted. There are others who may be socially awkward and find it difficult to be social or to assert themselves. We must be aware that a certain amount of fragility exists - therefore, we must be mindful of our words and actions toward them.

Self-efficacy refers to an individual's belief in his or her capacity to execute behaviors necessary to produce specific performance attainments (Bandura, 1997). Self-efficacy reflects confidence in the ability to exert control over one's own motivation, behavior, and social environment. As educators, we are tasked not only with teaching self-efficacy to our students, but also modeling the behavior transparently, and unfortunately we don't often address the lack of self-efficacy that exists among our teaching population.

For those who are not confident communicators, developing new skills is important. Being committed to trying new things, engaging in new behaviors and developing a greater sense of self-awareness, self-importance, and ultimately, self-management needs to be part of an individual's personal and professional development plan.

Observing others through peer observations, creating opportunities to improve performance, setting "stretch goals" to motivate achievement, and celebrating successes are examples of improving self-efficacy.

As colleagues and leaders, we can do our very best to be patient, attempt to model the behavior or outcome that we want, and also hold those individuals accountable.

Some people are naturally introverted, may be shy or may simply lack confidence based on lack of experience. If this is the case, leaders can support and encourage them to get out of their shells. I suggest some cooperative learning training, or improv for teachers, which is similar to what a theatre student would experience. They could join Toastmasters or take other experiential learning classes to assist them in better communication.

Through developing interpersonal skills,
and engaging in social interaction
over time, educators can improve their own
self-efficacy. By doing so, they will demonstrate
achievement, confidence and success for
students as well.

Energy Vampires

Dealing with misaligned energy vampires who suck the life out of the room requires being intentional, even though it's difficult - because they are difficult.

As educators, our focus should be the students and what's best for them. Some people are going to take whatever is said personally and/or negatively. I give these people the least amount of attention because when I think of the organizational culture of the school, I tend to put more energy into those educators whose mission and vision is in alignment with the organization.

An *energy vampire* is a person who enjoys undermining authority, has no thought for the organizational goals (what's best for students), and revels in negativity. I restrict their influence because they could be detrimental to the organization, like weeds. By keeping them restricted, they have less opportunities to negatively influence other people. They aren't sponsors or department heads, they aren't the chair for the holiday party or head of the courtesy committee. They aren't leading anything, and that's intentional.

When possible, I coach them up, observe them frequently and provide feedback. Sometimes that works. When it doesn't, I coach them out. They find other opportunities that are better suited for them because hopefully, over time those *energy vampires* see that they are not in alignment and are ready to go anyway.

Burnout Is Real, What You Do About It Matters

"A state of emotional, physical and mental exhaustion caused by excessive and prolonged stress. It occurs when you feel overwhelmed, emotionally drained, and unable to meet constant demands."

Signs of Burnout

Based on the definition of burnout, every single person who has worked in education has likely been in a temporary state of burnout at various points throughout the school year. It can come and go. It typically happens before Christmas break, and we come back rejuvenated after Spring Break, then boom, testing and here we go again. This happens with students too. You'll see heightened levels of discipline, excitement, emotions all over the place...

After Christmas and Spring Breaks, I do a school reset and go over expectations, procedures and have grade level meetings. This helps shift the focus and helps everyone be clear about school-wide expectations. It helps everyone.

Suggested Activities: If one staff member is burned out, likely there are more. Be intentional about changing the energy, culture and climate within your staff. Things you can do: Provide lunch for your staff just because. In lieu of the traditional staff meeting, do team building activities and games, go on a bowling outing, or do lip sync battles or talent shows – including giving feedback like Simon on *America's Got Talent*. These types of activities can boost morale and be the energy increase needed to propel them through the feelings of exhaustion or stress they are experiencing.

When an educator is experiencing burnout, there may be a glaring difference in their attendance. Their physical appearance can change – it could be weight gain, weight loss or maybe even a skin outbreak. They tend to be very impatient, snappy. That results in having more referrals and more discipline issues in the classroom. They aren't part of the school community. They used to be a sponsor or actively involved, and now their contribution is minimal. They tend to be more pessimistic. They could be more emotional with frustration being the baseline, with bursts of anger and even tears. The education could be disorganized, evidenced by the physical appearance of the classroom, desk or even losing the student's work. They leave right when the bell rings; they are not staying around.

It's the responsibility of the team to recognize when a colleague is in this space. They need support and that begins with a conversation. The leader could do a wellness check – simply a one-on-one meeting, no phone, no computer, and simply ask, "How are you doing?" "What can I do to support you?" So as basic as that sounds, that doesn't happen often enough. We will see these educators, take their behavior personally, and fail to ask them how they are doing, we just won't do it.

Listen to the teachers and give them what they ask for – the things that are feasible. Sometimes it has nothing to do with school and the work. It may be,

I'm going through a divorce, I'm having financial problems, my parent was diagnosed with such and such disease, my therapy dog is dying, I'm trying to get pregnant and I can't, my partner left me and I can't seem to get it together, I'm trying to get a second job because I'm the sole bread winner and my salary isn't enough. Some teachers are over-extended at school and have taken on too much outside of their classroom, some don't leave work at a reasonable time – staying until 6 pm – they have good intentions, but may not be planning properly.

Instead of doing wellness checks and helping them strategize, we take it personally when they drop off committees and no longer want to sponsor a group, or they made one or two negative comments in a staff meeting. So this is where we go into "Super principal I'm going to write you up mode," because how dare you! "I'm not like your last principals, they were too nice!" "I'm not going to coddle you!" "You all are just acting like babies!" Gosh! We have a lot to learn.

When the leader starts treating the employee like that, they get disgruntled and really feel like crap.

Their attendance becomes more sporadic. They were already burnt out and now you started contributing to that. In order for the leader to have a wellness check, and be candid and transparent, the leader must have modeled that behavior and have a relationship/ rapport with that person in order for them to actually share what's happening.

Have you modeled vulnerability/transparency with your team? I don't have to do a survey to know *the answer is "No" for most leaders.*

My Own Burnout

When my mom went into cardiac arrest, I was on the Family and Medical Leave Act (FMLA) and began to miss partial days. I didn't want to tell the staff I was out because I didn't want them to think things would fall apart... because in my mind I was thinking they would believe the school wouldn't be run in the same manner if I wasn't there, and start to panic. I was just being private and weird. I had to check myself and trust my team. Things were not going to fall apart, and I needed them to know I wasn't there because I needed them to be more vigilant in my absence. I wanted everybody to work together as a team. You may be thinking, "Shouldn't that happen anyway?" Yes, but I had never asked them to help in this way. I was stressing about what was happening in the building while I was at the hospital with my mom, wondering what was happening with my assistant principal, wondering if he was getting help, causing unnecessary stress. Had I initially disclosed and asked for help in the first place, it would have made it a lot easier.

This was a short-lived two-week window of my behavior. Then in a staff meeting, I was candid about what was going on with my mom, explained I was on FMLA and I specifically asked for support in the hallways, in the cafeteria and to minimize the use of hall passes unless it was important. Those were ways to help control the daily operations of the school day in my absence. That was a breaking point because I'm humorous, that's a given. I do talk to my staff, but I shared very little about me personally. That moment of transparency showed I was a human being, struggling like they were. Being in the hospital every night and coming to work in the mornings was difficult. When they heard what was happening, they were very supportive of me.

Unappreciated – Show Gratitude, Celebrate Them

Overwhelmed? When you notice they are feeling overwhelmed, do the heart work necessary to validate them and their current state. A good way to start is by asking how you can support them and by listening to what they are saying and not saying. Then support him/her in creating an action plan, feasibility plan or simply offering to be patient as they are working through the challenges, especially if they are having personal issues that are contributing to the overwhelm. It is not all the responsibility of the building administrator. If your assistant principal has a better relationship with that staff member, then ask them to step in. Be realistic, if you don't have the relationship but someone else does, step aside and invite them to support the situation.

Questioning if They Are in the Right Profession

It takes a strong person to recognize that they are no longer suited for education. Even if they haven't said the words but are leading to that, a conversation can go like this, "It's okay to walk away from a situation that you may not be equipped for. It doesn't make you a failure or a bad person, and I appreciate you for recognizing that it's a misalignment with the thing you are passionate about, and the thing you are actually doing." Thank them for the time they have given and for standing in the gap with us who are doing this work, and offer to write a letter of recommendation. Don't judge them. To the world, it may be shocking but that person knew in the first two or three years that they weren't in the right place. I appreciate that about them; it takes guts and courage. It's not a sign of weakness. It's better to deal with it early than to spend 15 years being miserable, knowing they are misplaced.

Right Profession, Difficult Times

Sometimes they need a reset and sometimes they need encouragement through what is missing. When that has happened, I've asked my leadership to come and just talk to them, encourage them, and let them know that someone other than me sees them and recognizes the work they are doing. Sometimes just coming by and saying hello goes a long way.

So I challenge you as leaders to take off the mask of superiority, perfectionism and don't be afraid to model vulnerability. Having those candid conversations in one-on-one meetings or in staff meetings where appropriate is critical, period.

Once we have insight as to what's happening with the educator, we must give room for that staff member to work through an action plan, whether the strategy or agreement is that they choose to see a therapist, attend some type of training or work with a staff member on developing some routines and procedures to help with their calendar. Giving room may mean some time off, suggesting they go to employee benefit services or offering to give them a break by covering their class for a bit (yes, you, the principal, back in the classroom). All of what we said about the staff member experiencing burnout applies to principals too – hopefully those little breaks won't add to your burnout if you covered 90 minutes of class for two days!)

It could be a temporary state or it may be time for a change. When we start feeling that way as educators, it's detrimental to us and ALL stakeholders can be in this crisis mode with us if we're not careful. And in my 20 years in this field, I've yet to have a professional development around what happens when an educator feels burnt-out.

Holistic Fitness for Educators

*How often do we put ourselves and our
personal needs on the back burner?*

To be effective and healthy, your physical, financial, emotional and mental well-being should be a priority.

Practice Healthy Eating (and Drinking) Habits

Oftentimes educators do not drink enough water or eat healthy because of time constraints or issues that might come up during the day. It's easy to forget to eat, or to choose something quick that's not necessarily healthy. And, the reality is, many teachers forgo drinking water so that they lessen the need to take restroom breaks. These are not healthy habits; they just seem to be "natural" choices made just to fit everything in.

Of course, exercising is important. There are many options. If you make it a priority, your body will thank you in the long run.

Balancing Finances Takes Discipline

Let's face it - finances affect our ability to care for ourselves and our families. When our finances are out of control, it causes stress. Nobody needs more stress, so if the lack of finances is an issue, please be proactive in doing something about them. Accounting is not my specialty, but since I'm an educator, you may know where I'm going with this...

For increasing your income in the long term: Consider furthering your education to get an increase in your pay! Many school districts make it easy for you to get advanced degrees (with tuition reimbursement). You may be thinking that you can't possibly add another thing to your already busy life, but you may be surprised with what you can handle. You must look at how this will benefit you in the long run.

For simple solutions: Create a budget and stick to it. Stop overspending. Cook meals at home and stop eating out. Buy a book by one of the financial gurus... whatever it is, you can do it if you face what's happening. If you need help putting a budget together, do not be afraid to ask for help. Do not get discouraged if you go over budget. Try better next month.

The economy continues to change. Do what you can to invest in your short-term and long-term financial needs. You deserve it.

Mental Health Issues Facing Educators

Recently a video was trending on the Internet of a 32-year-old female teacher punching and then stomping a special needs student. It was jarring, to say the least. As I watched, I knew there was more to it than this single incident. It was traumatizing and extremely violent, yet I fully believe it was not premeditated nor intentional. It was uncomfortable to watch because it goes against everything I was taught and believe about the role of the teacher. I was always taught that a teacher should never put their hands on a student. The teacher should exercise the absolute highest degree of emotional and physical restraints.

Reflecting on my beliefs, I lacked the compassion and empathy for teachers that faced emotional struggles. I was not able to identify with such behaviors. It didn't take much to realize that something snapped in the teacher – she was triggered from some previous experience/trauma, and/or had her own mental health issues which prevented her from being rational.

We must be mindful that all educators are human and we each face our own emotional encounters. While I do not condone an adult harming a student, it should be noted that adults need the same emotional support as students.

During the hiring process, we fail to screen for emotional or social skill deficiencies. As school personnel, we can observe behaviors and there are some warning signs:

- Quick temper

- Irrational behaviors such as crying hysterically or hitting a wall

- Making assumptions that are known to be false

- Attendance Concerns

- Uncontrolled sleeping incidences

It is imperative that adults working with young people need continued therapeutic support. This is one of the reasons why the need to build and sustain authentic relationships are important.

Self-care Tips

- Drink plenty of water

- Eat healthy

- Get adequate sleep

- Journaling; writing experiences, thoughts and emotions can be freeing and liberating

- Take small mental health breaks during the day

- Say no

- Don't overcommit

- Take bubble baths

- Meditate or join a church or community center

Demonstrating Appreciation

Appreciation goes a long way! It's essential to morale, and it's the right thing to do!

If you are an administrator, ask yourself, "What would have made me happy as a teacher in meetings?" Then do that for teachers, or get suggestions from social media if you are unsure.

Focus on the goal - appreciating them, not being limited by a budget - being creative or simply saying "I appreciate you" doesn't cost anything!

Conference Room Service

During Parent-Teacher Conferences, we created a "Room Service" experience for the teachers. I went to the store, bought different types of snacks and gallon sized plastic bags. We sent the students around with "Conference Room Cards" which allowed the teachers to mark the kind of snack/ beverage they preferred. Then the students and I put the bags together and then delivered them. I wanted the teachers to not only know, but also feel appreciated. Catering to and serving them was a way to express how much they are valued. The teachers really seemed to enjoy being catered to, and we got great satisfaction in seeing them happy. That venture cost me $50 out of pocket and I got the idea from Pinterest.

Be Aware of Time

Days go so quickly in the classroom and often teachers find themselves "out of time" when they need to prep, grade papers or complete projects essential to their duties. I've found that giving "the gift of time" when possible allows them the chance to catch up. Sometimes catching up may be simply breathing, taking a restroom break, grabbing a snack in the lounge, and gathering their thoughts. Record keeping time, and the opportunity to work in the classroom without students present, is invaluable! Time matters. Especially when I schedule meetings,

I try to offer fun activities which are engaging and give them a chance to unwind. We've done things like human fuse ball and having lip sync battles. Because I have a big personality and enjoy having fun, spearheading these types of activities is right up my alley, and work well with the faculty at a visual and performing arts school.

However, all schools and faculty are different and therefore, it's important to be creative and care for your staff in ways they will enjoy. So, when you think of meetings, be aware of what time of day you schedule them, how long they are, and how you use the time. The reality? Who feels like they just 'need' another meeting? Yet, how many try and fit information into every second of scheduled meetings, and even go over the allotted time? Don't do that! Be respectful of time, focus on what's important, and if there is an extra five or fifteen minutes left, and you're actually done, dismiss them so they can use that time to rejuvenate and/or do other essential things to support themselves, the students and ultimately, the organization.

Compensating in Other Ways

Unfortunately, there are certain realities that we as leaders can't easily overcome, and often salaries are one of those things. Think about our secretaries. They usually get paid the least and often feel like they don't matter. Yet, they are the first point of contact! Their roles are vital to the operation and function of the school. Parents call them. Kids visit them. Administration relies on them. A dedicated secretary not only keeps things orderly, but she also protects those she serves, including those to whom they report. So be sure and show them how much you appreciate them. Ask them questions about how you can support them, give them respect, courtesy and care.

If there are things you can do to free up their time occasionally, do them. And, get them a cup of coffee once in a while, especially if you've been acting like you forgot how to do that yourself!

With intention, planning and effective implement-ation, schools can also create equity by providing an environment where all staff can be successful

- Bring in community-based organizations trained in restorative justice practices

- Care Team Meetings

- Healing Circles

- Social Skills Training

- Anger Management Training

- Staff Peace Rooms

  Practice courtesy and appreciation.

Check the Source

Though the halls may chatter, pay attention to what you're filtering.

In leadership, everyone wants to tell you something. The reality is that people gossip. A turtle can't accurately tell a story about a giraffe because his perspective (height) is limited.

Beware of Poison! Checking the source helps to diffuse situations because, when the perspective is tainted or jaded, bad intentions can cause confusion. You run the risk of losing credibility if you "run wild" with misinformation. Conflict can cause personal and professional damage to everyone.

Checking the Source Means Considering All Parties and their Perspectives

- Parents

- Teachers/Staff

- Students

- Central Office/Districts

Each of us must be mindful not to make hasty/emotional decisions without qualifying/ checking the source.

Dr. Shahid's Climate and Culture Overview with Questionnaire

*The Climate and Culture of the school is
the heartbeat or the brain of the organization.
From there, you can observe, diagnose,
address, create and implement a
plan of action toward success.*

Climate and Culture **Drive the Failure or Success of the School**

When the environment is toxic, you can feel, see, smell, hear it and almost taste it. A toxic environment hits all senses. It could be the way the students are approached by safety officers, or served by cafeteria workers. You can walk into the cafeteria and feel tension; you can walk the halls and not see teachers present. You can hear the level of disrespect – profanity, aggressive tones or voices. You can see kids in areas where they shouldn't be – unauthorized stairways or exits. In some cases, physical altercations occur readily and repeatedly because adults aren't present. You can smell marijuana with older students or urine in elementary schools – where the restrooms haven't been cleaned, trash may have stayed overnight or unpleasant body odor. You will see trash, littering or graffiti in common areas. And, in a toxic environment, you won't often see artwork – because kids don't respect the space enough to have the building print-rich, and teachers don't value the student's work so they don't post it, or leave it up for months.

Creating and Maintaining a Healthy, Productive and Positive Climate and Culture

Culture and Climate drives the success of a school. You know if it's a positive culture within 30 seconds of being in the building. You can tell by the attitudes, behaviors and communication of the students, and how the school conducts business (the routines and procedures). It's how the building smells; it's how adults are talking to kids and how kids are talking to each other. It's how the leader talks to everybody – teachers, parents, students.

The way the leader looks and behaves can affect the culture as well.

Is the leader anxious, disheveled, sloppy, or nervous?

Is the leader confident, poised, an open communicator, supportive, and energetic?

Is the leader visible and approachable?

Walking around with a cup of coffee in your hand doesn't look good, nor does it equate to productivity. It means that your hands are not free to jump in when needed. If you think about it, it's kind of unprofessional to do hall duty with coffee in your hand, while sitting at your desk is more appropriate.

A Healthy Climate and Culture Necessitates Intention and Engagement from Everyone

The daily operation plan should be a time stamped document that accounts for every hour or scheduled by breakfast, lunch or dismissal. The crucial piece is team accountability. The leader should know where the team is and what they are doing. From the assistant principal to the secretary, the team interacting and functioning effectively together is critical to the culture as well.

Dr. Shahid's Climate and Culture Questionnaire

Here's a sample document that can be used intact or as a guide to tailoring an appropriate questionnaire for your classroom or school. Questionnaires can be anonymous or personalized, depending on the type of data you wish to capture, and what you intend to do with the information you gather.

Parents:

Do you feel welcome at your child's school?

Does the school provide regular and effective communication to parents?

Do you have input in your child's academic or discipline plan?

Have you received positive communication regarding your child's progress?

Does your school provide/suggest resources for families in transition?

Do you have a relationship with your child's principal?

How often do you receive communication when your child is misbehaving and making poor decisions?

Do you feel that your child is safe at school?

Does your child have respectful relationships with more than two adults at the school?

Who can your child talk to if they are experiencing emotional/physical challenges at school?

Students:

Do you have positive relationships with the staff in your building?

When you are experiencing difficulties, do you have a trusted adult you can talk to at your school?

Do you feel safe at school?

Are there opportunities for students to talk with school leaders regarding ideas, issues or concerns?

Do you feel like you are accepted at your school/in classroom?

Are you giving opportunities to correct assignments and master objectives if they have been missed?

Do you miss your teachers and/or friends when you are not at school?

Staff:

Do you have positive relationships with your colleagues?

When you are experiencing difficulties, do you have a trusted colleague you can talk to at your school?

Do you feel safe at school?

Are there opportunities for staff to talk with the Administrative team regarding ideas, issues or concerns?

Do you feel a sense of mutual respect at your school?

Do you feel valued and appreciated by your school/ district leadership team?

Is your attendance rate below 85%?

Conclusion

"I raised you to be a thoroughbred. When thoroughbreds run they wear blinders to keep their eyes focused straight ahead with no distractions, no other horses. They hear the crowd but they do not listen. They just run their own race."

~ "The Right Words at the Right Time"
by Marlo Thomas

Before my daughter began her 800-meter race, I would hear her coach say, "Drive Phase" and "Run Your Race." I understood that to mean two things: stay focused on the ground immediately in front of you and work *YOUR* plan.

We spend more time judging and comparing ourselves to one another instead of minding our own business. As we run toward our professional endeavors, we cannot turn our heads to the left or to the right. Checking out someone else's race or chasing perceived success leads to professional suicide.

In *Know Your Place, Run Your Race* I offer practical nuggets to challenge the readers to self-examine their own strengths and weaknesses. I encourage the reader by making it clear that we are all leaders despite our titles, positions or salaries. We have the ability to make valuable contributions and be of influence in this journey of educating, teaching and learning.

It has taken me many years to get the courage to write a book for educators. I allowed fear and criticism from others to defer my goals. I have learned that it takes courageous and vulnerable leaders to remove the masks and blinders. *Run Your Race* means not allowing fear and self-doubt to deter you from your dreams. Yes, traumatic events can cause emotional strain and can have long-term effects. But when we are honest and transparent about our experiences, healing can occur. Then we can experience true joy and execute whatever plan is before us.

I challenge other educators to get in the game and share their stories or nuggets of wisdom– the reason that we go to conferences is to learn from others. *Newsflash!* Not all conference presenters are educators. Some presenters may lack your expertise and experience. On the other hand, they are not afraid to share their stories of success/failures and they are confident in what they are able to offer. Being an educator is a noble profession, but we must understand our worth, value, and be willing to share our experiences.

We can learn so much from each other, and we need each other. I am challenging you to get out of your own way, to step up and *Run Your Race* even if you have to do it afraid!

RESOURCES

A resource is something that
can be used for a purpose.
The following book lists are excellent
resources for educators and parents.

Dr. Shahid's Recommended Books for Educators

"Between the World and Me" by Ta-Nehisi Coates

This book is a letter to the author's 15-year-old son. Coates describes his personal, historical and intellectual development and how to live in a Black body in America. He also illustrates the importance of Black people being in their community, finding joy and understanding that the struggle is hard, but it provides meaning in this life.

"The Power of Focus" by Jack Canfield, Les Hewitt and Mark Victor Hansen

I love this book because it talks about how the majority of people struggle professionally and personally because of lack of focus. The authors do an excellent job of outlining 10 steps to help you focus and inspire you to take action.

"My Grandmother's Hands" by Resemaa Menakem

This book is about racialized trauma and the effects that it has had on the body. It is a call to action for Americans to recognize that racism is not only about the head but also the body. The author takes you through a step-by-step healing process based on the latest neuroscience healing methods.

"Leverage Leadership" by Paul Bambrick-Santoyo

I love this book because it really addresses what sets school leaders apart.

It postulates exceptional school leaders succeed because of how they use their time. I love this book because it really addresses the skills that set exemplary school leaders apart, with the author explaining they succeed by consistently using seven core principles or levers to maximize every minute of their day.

"If You Don't Feed the Teachers They Eat the Students!" Guide to Success for Administrators and Teachers by Neila A. Conners

This book really offers pointers on how to show your staff you appreciate them without spending a ton of money.

"The Students Are Watching: Schools and the Moral Contract" by Theodore and Nancy Sizer

Every school leader should read this thought-provoking book. It explores why schools struggle to connect with students, what schools are failing to do, and what they need to do differently. This book really focuses on schools being a place where relationships are paramount. The Sizers stress that if we cannot understand and build strong relationships with the child, we cannot effectively educate him or her. It is not enough to focus on the academic content alone.

'The Big Picture: Education is Everyone's Business" by Dennis Littky with Samantha Grabelle

This book is very inspiring for parents, teachers and administrators. The book details the success of The Met, a character school in Rhode Island. Through its innovative approach, the school was able to tap into the passion and interest of the students. This book challenges the way we view the current educational systems and encourages disruptive innovation.

Dr. Shahid's Recommended Books for Young Adults

"Rainbow Jordan" by Alice Childress

I read this book as a teenager and could relate to the main character in more ways than one. This book is about a 14-year-old African-American girl who was in and out of foster care. It illustrates the struggles of growing up poor and the trauma associated with that lifestyle. It is a story of hope and resilience.

"To Be Popular or Smart" by Dr. Jawanza Kunjufu

This is a great read for young people, educators and parents looking to get information on peer pressure. It asks the question: How can we give youth the same confidence in academics as they experience in athletics and the arts?

Favorite Quote: *"We must demand excellence of ourselves and agitate and advocate justice from the larger society."*

"The Hate You Give" by Angie Thomas

I love this book because of the social and political message it sends. Starr Carter, the lead character, is an inspiration to girls trying to find their voice.

Favorite Quote: *"What's the point of having the voice if you're going to be silent in those moments you shouldn't be?"*

"Outliers" by Malcolm Gladwell

This nonfiction book examines achievement and failure, and how people achieve success through practice and opportunity and the help of others.

Favorite Quote: *"Practice isn't the thing you do once you're good. It's the thing you do that makes you good."*

The Skin I'm In by Sharon Flake

This book deals with the struggle of low self-esteem that many Black girls face when they're darker skinned.

Favorite Quote: *"To look in the mirror and like what you see, even when it doesn't look like your idea of beauty."*

About the Author

Kacy Seals, Ed. D.

Kacy obtained a Bachelor of Arts degree in Business Administration from Clark Atlanta University in Atlanta, GA in 1995. She soon realized that educating, inspiring and coaching young people was her mission and calling. It was this calling that allowed her to transition from substitute teacher to principal in a six-year period.

Kacy resolved not to allow her demographics to determine her destiny. She did not allow a childhood impeded by homelessness and drug abuse deter her from pursuing her purpose. She overcame various societal ills and turned her stumbling blocks into stepping stones. Today, that spirit of endurance guides and fosters her relationship with the students she serves, many of whom share similar experiences and stories.

She believes resiliency is the capacity to successfully overcome the effects of a high-risk environment and develop social competence despite exposure to severe stress. Her greatest contribution as a principal has been sharing her own personal journey with both her students and staff. Kacy believes that the work of educating children is everyone's business, which she describes as "heart work" not "hard work." She considers herself an educator who is led by her faith and the notion that failure is not an option.

She believes that our personal triumph may be the only proof that we can become great. This personal mantra has allowed her to go beyond the classroom walls when she started her own educational con-sulting business "Through the Eyes of a Child, LLC." Kacy has presented at various conferences and universities on *The Common Factors Related to Resiliency that Impact the Academic and Social Success of At-Risk High School Students.*

Always driven, Kacy added another milestone to her life's journey in 2012 when she received her Educational Doctorate degree from Maryville Univer-sity. On the road to her doctorate, as a principal, teacher and lecturer, she received numerous accolades such as: 2008 Aspiring New Principal Award from the Missouri Association of Secondary Schools, 2011 Pettus Principal of the Year Award, SASSP 2016 Exemplary Principal of the Year, 2017 St. Louis American Excellence In Education Recipient, and 2018 St. Louis Public Principal of the Year.

As principal of Central Visual and Performing Arts High School, her alma mater, Kacy understands the power of walking in your season and not taking your assignment lightly. Her confidence and audacity continue to help foster an environment that builds leadership capacity among both students and staff. She is determined to be an example of a courageous and fearless leader by sustaining the schools' values, traditions and commitment to excellence.

Kacy resides in St. Louis, Missouri with her husband Mellve, three daughters - Kennedy, Kori, Kyndal and her bonus son Mellve III.

DrKacyShahid.com